Woods,
A MUSICAL PATH

JANE SUMMERS

authorHOUSE®

AuthorHouse™
1663 Liberty Drive
Bloomington, IN 47403
www.authorhouse.com
Phone: 833-262-8899

Published by AuthorHouse 11/16/2022

ISBN: 978-1-6655-7519-5 (sc)
ISBN: 978-1-6655-7518-8 (e)

CONTENTS

Section 2: Musical Album, Spring Revoir.

Section 3: Bavavovue in Durvue

Section 4: Prayers in new language Durvue.

ACKNOWLEDGEMENTS

This book is dedicated to my father Dr. Chinta Chidananda Rao (Chief Medical Officer, South Central Railway), my mother Chinta Visalakshi, my husband Srinivas Madiraju, my daughter Anika Madiraju, my family and friends.

My sincere appreciation to all my friends, and well-wishers who have helped me at all times. I am grateful and thankful for all their help.

PREFACE

Jane Summers Commemorative Coin

Awards received for the year 2022.

https://www.24-7pressrelease.com/press-release/494891/marquis-whos-who-selects-durga-madiraju-for-excell!ence-in-software-engineering-information-technology-and-arts-and-entertainment

Marquis Top Artist Award

https://www.google.com/amp/s/marquistopartists.com/2022/09/05/durga-madiraju/amp/

SECTION 1
75 POEMS

1. WOODS, A PATH OF FLOWERS

Woods, a path
I take, every day, a season,
A path of summer flowers!
A summer,
A path a difference
A color of woods!
An art, I paint
Several, canvases!
A decor, my mind!
My thoughts,
For a difference
Of an art
Every day!
An art, my mind, I need
For a peace, my mind, a calm!

For a peace, my mind, a solitude
For a grace, I dress, a flower,
For a walk, my gestures, a season, a tree,
For a dance, I walk, a season, a breeze!

Woods, a path
I take,
Only for a smile,
I need every day!
Only A cheer,
I need to exude,
Every day!
Only a grace,
I need to gather,
Every Season!
Not to earn,
A name,
A frowny, unkempt,

A shabby dowdy ma'm,
Thy name!

Oh Woods,
How mysterious,
thou art!
Only a smile,
My lips,
Every!
My woods,
Only a grace,
Only a mystery,
A smile,
Every path!

Oh Woods,
You are the one I love!
Woods, thy Mystery,
A smile,
Every!

2. PRIMROSES, MY PROMISES

Primroses, a new season,
A spring every year!
Promises,
I await,
To fulfill,
A color, for an art
I fulfill,
Every year!

A color,
I did not see, new
A color,
I relate,
For several!
My woods! I did not see,
A path, new,
A path,
Not visible,
Unless!

A path,
I grow,
A use,
Several,
A path I wear
Every season,
For a difference!

3. A DAUGHTER, NOT ANY A FLAW!

A daughter precious every day,
Every season.
Not any a flaw, a mother's eyes.
A mother only for a difference,
Of A love and wisdom,
A daughter I do not ever fault for a flaw.
A daughter more beautiful everyday,
Her kindness and gestures only
A match!
A mother,
Everyday only for a fulfillment, all!
completed with a grace,
With no fault or flaws!
A learning of a daughter,
Only for a best!
Not any, a lacking for!
A mother, a view of a daughter,
A view,
Inside and outside,
Only for a view safe, precious, graceful,
Of a daughter!
Peace and harmony all days,
A daughter and a mother!
Never a fear, only a joy, every day!
A mother only happy any a age.
A grace, a blend,
A harmony, a mother and a daughter!
Mother a gift, of a daughter
Daughter, a gift priceless, a mother,
A gift, a lifetime!

4. A CONVERSATION OF A WINDOW

A conversation
Of a window,
Several, windows,
Of conversations!
A need of something,
A need of someone!
A conversation of a celebration,
A cheer of a festival,
A cheer of a happiness,
exude,
An accolade,
I need to shout,
A joy!

A conversation,
For a dress,
A grace,
I need to show,
An appreciation
I need
For a happiness,
I share!

A conversation
Of a disharmony,
I need to share,
For a guidance,
Of A view of a door,

A conversation Any,
Only for a use,
Any a place,
A day Of cheer
Only I need!

5. MY EYES, I SEEK, FOR A DIFFERENCE EVERY!

My eyes,
I seek,
Every,
A need everyday,
I fulfill!
A difference, for a new better!
A cheer, I need every day,
I fulfill, a difference, for a learning
A view,
I share!
My eyes,
I see
Only
For a difference, a new,
a new color, I seek, every,
Only To share,
My difference!
My eyes,
I seek!
I found!
A new, a learning,
A value!

6. WOODS, A TRAIL OF FLOWERS!

Woods, a trail,
Flowers, a path, every,
A harmony, a shape!
A grace, colors, similars!
A trail of flowers,
A dance, a gesture,
An expression
A breeze,
A harmony of a dance!
A flower,
My eyes, my Iris,
A season I wear!
A grace,
A smile,
A sorrow,
A flower downcast,
Woods,
Only
A trail of flowers,
A grace,
Every season!
Colors
My eyes,
I need,
A joy,
Of a season,
A happiness,
My day!

7. WOODS, A TRAIL OF TREES!

Woods,
A trail of trees,
So many expressions,
Profiles,
Definitions,
Characteristics!
Several
I need to
Mark,
For a difference,
A day,
A season!

Woods,
A trail of trees,
I see,
Similar,
New, some
A season!
A season,
I need,
A few days,
Only to mark,
My work,
Only for better!
A difference,
I mark,
an area of my work
For a new progress,
A new level,
A branch,
Higher,
A trail of trees,
I need to only

9

Know,
A New every!

Oh, Woods,
A trail of trees,
I appreciate, you
I celebrate you
Every year!

For A new, I gather, And
A new
You are true!
I am celebrated!
A new knowledge, true!
A new season, true!
A lifetime!

8. WOODS, A PATH, A SOLITUDE!

Oh Woods,
A path,
I always see,
To compare!
A tree,
With no breeze, A calm,
A silence,
A calm,
Only, I match my woods!
My trees,
I see next day,
Because of a calm!

My trees,
An anger,
A breeze, violent
My leaves,
Only a shake,
My leaves, a
Fall down,
A grace!
Until rain!
A calmness,
A joy,
A celebration my rain!
My leaves,
My flowers,
Afresh, a tree!

An anger,
I do not need to exude,
A sorrow or a regret,
To follow,
A wrath of words or others
A celebration,
A togetherness,
My trees, I match

A character,
A definition,
I need to create!
An art,
A pattern,
Every day,
Until
A day of happiness,
Joy,
Is true!
A living,
A cheer, a joy!

Oh, woods,
I only understand you everyday,
Not a wrath or a quarrel,
Only a calm, a smile
Every!

9. WOODS FOR A DAY!

Woods,
a day,
I walk,
Away from my
Everyday,
A walk slow,
An appreciation true,
A walk fast,
To gather,
My thoughts,
A peace,
I need,
To move away to a
Path of harmony!

Woods,
I walk a day,
For a purpose,
I need to gather flowers,
Leaves for an art,
A search of a path,
For a completion!
To hurry back,
My home,
Only a need!
To start my art!
Woods, a walk,
I need to carve for a purpose Of a rest!
A need,
A hurry,
I need to set aside
For peace and harmony,
Woods, A walk, A path True!

Sincerity,
Devotion,
A day
For a day of rest!

10.   WOODS, A LEAF, A LIFE!

Woods,
Several leaves,
Several branches, a day!
A leaf,
A few
Only a glance,
I see,
For a day

A few,
A branch,
I did not glance at,
For ignorance!

A leaf
A color similar, all,
A shape, a pattern similar all!
An ignorance
I am unaware!
I need to know the leaves,
A branch higher,
Only for a knowledge,
To appreciate the beauty,
Shape, pattern, color,
Atop, a tree,
A grace
A leaf,
A path,
I walk!
To gain,
A Knowledge,
I did not know,
A difference, a truth,
A new, a need,

For a harmony,
Only to remove
Differences,
Seasons!

11.   WOODS, A PATH, FOR A BEST!

Woods,
I walk, a path,
A season,
A seasons's best,
For fruits, flowers
And leaves,
I pick, an autumn!

Woods,
I see, a summer afar,
A path,
I walk for a best, a summer!
To gather summer flowers,
A day for a fragrance,
A rose!
A lavender,
A cleanliness, a fragrance,
A smell I inhale, afresh, a health!
A mum, a fragrance,
I place before God,
For a worship,
My prayers of moon,
A fragrance!
My,
Traditions,
Customs
Only a need,
A peace and harmony,
My day!
Woods, A path, I pick!

A best,
I see,
Seasons, every,
A smile,
My day!

A cheer,
A joy,
I want to exude around,
For never a fault
Of unhappiness!

12.   I DID NOT KNOW, NOT AN ANSWER!

Woods,
I seek to ask
Thy a question?
An autumn fall of leaves!
When is autumn?
Not an answer,
I did not know!

I need to know,
An answer for queries,
Only,
I need to seek,
Books,
Remove word living
Living
For answers,
I need to know!

I sought an answer,
A disappointment,
Late, but never too late,
Only I tried, a next and next,
Success is my name!

I only seek now,
Answers!
To Questions,
An ignorance,
I was not
Aware of!

An ignorance,
I did not know,
Not an answer!
A question,
I do not know,
Not an answer!

An answer,
I find
In my book!

13.   A PATH I WALK FOR A GRACE!

A path I walk
Only for a stalk,
Only to compare,
Only for a disgrace
Of Another,
But Not for a grace,
A walk of stalk,
I do not need!
To abandon,
Only a joy!

A path
I walk
Only to
Find fault
Of another
For a decline,
A path I walk
Only to say
I am better
Not you!
A path of walk
I must abandon,
A path of walk,
I must walk
only for a grace,
A joy!

A path of walk
A grace I walk,
A walk of friendship,
I share, a conversation!

14. WOODS, A CONVERSATION, A JOY!

Woods,
A conversation,
A joy!
Woods,
A walk,
A joy,
A walk, a path!

A conversation,
Trees, similar,
A harmony of a day,
Leaves calm,
A patience
I exude, a day!
A conversation of my
Studies and work,
A patience,
I exude
For a result!

Leaves a shake,
A new,
A learning new
In my life!

A conversation,
With woods,
A need I need to know
And understand better For success!
Results, my truth,
A success or a failure
A conversation
Of a result!

15. WOODS, A HARVEST I CELEBRATE

Woods,
A devotion today!
A day I
Need to celebrate,
A harvest,
Vegetables,
Green leaves,
Fruits,
Flowers,
You bestowed
Every season!

Today I celebrate,
A festival of harvest,
Sankranti,
A pongal,
I make,
Rice, butter, cardamom, dry fruits and sugar,
A pongal dish!

A Pongal Festival!
A Health, Happiness, Prosperity
Of my family, Friends,
And others,
I pray for!

16. WOODS, A PATH, MY DEVOTION

Woods,
I walk a path,
Only for a devotion,
A peace and calm,
I need to unfold,
A devotion
Of someone,
In my life!
My parents,
Teachers,
Remember,
For the knowledge
Hard work
I need a devotion for!

Woods,
A devotion,
A sincerity,
Of my learning, true!
Blessings
Of my teachers, true!

A knowledge,
A learning,
Bestowed!

Woods,
A path of my devotion,
Sincere, loyal, kind,
A path of devotion I pray for every day!

17. WOODS A PATH, A FARM

Woods, a path
A farm,
I did not see!
A farm,
Fresh, vegetables,
Amidst woods,
Roses, daisies, mums,
A border, a grace
My farm!

Woods,
Only green,
Every A day,
A joy,
Woods!

Several farms,
Amidst woods,
Several Cottages
Only a town!

Oh, Woods!
A village,
Amidst woods,
I walk my woods
Around my village every day!

18. AN ODE TO A FARMER

A farmer,
Alone, a farm,
A devotion
To a farm,
Days and nights
Only for a harvest!

A sunrise prayer,
Early Dawn,
Prayers for
A day of hard work,
A day I need to clean a farm
Days of ploughing a farm
To make afresh a soil,
To mix a soil,
A harvest I ready, a soil, for!
A day I need to sow seeds of harvest,
And till my land!
A farmer,
A farm,
A harvest ready, a need

An ode,
I write, a few,
A farmer,
Sincere,
Devoted,
Not a day of work
Shunned,
Not A day of prayers missed!
A devotion true, every a day,
Thoust prayers blessed,
Not one

Every, a year,
Only prosperous,
Thy family!
A harvest,
A celebration
Every autumn,
Every Spring!

An ode
I sing every season
A farmer!
A farmer I am
I Reap rewards of harvest
A bountiful harvest I share
Every!

A prayer of a farmer
A devotion of a farmer,
I praise I sing,
A prayer,
An ode to a farmer,
A prayer I chant at,
A season, a day every,
True, a devotion!
True, a harvest!
Peace and harmony!
A farmer
And a farm!

An ode to a farmer!

19.   A FARM, I WALK WITH MY DAUGHTER!

A farm
I walk with
My daughter
An autumn!
A skirt faded
A color corn,
A faded white,
Sleeves a puff,
A three quarters!

Mother and daughter
A match of
A dress and color,
An autumn corn white dress,
A promise of an autumn sacred,
Days, sacred and happy!

An autumn bag
Dry corn leaves stuffed inside
An autumn apple, autumn squash,
For an autumn meal,
Walk down an autumn maze farm!

A conversation
Around a day of an autumn decor
Of an autumn corn art!
Smiles of autumn only a cheer,
A mother and daughter!
An autumn art,
An autumn walk,
A late afternoon,

Of A day in an autumn corn maze farm!
An autumn walk,
An autumn day,
A day of an autumn true!

20.   TEA, A GRACE OF WOODS

Tea, A grace,
An afternoon walk of woods,
A quench for a tea,
Scones and rasp berry buns,
My tea snacks
Of an afternoon
Tea time!

Buns,
Hot,
Currant,
A few a fruit
Only for a taste
Delicious, scrumptious,
A treat,
An afternoon tea walk!

A grace,
A tea,
My afternoon teatime!

Woods
Only a reminder,
A tea walk
Of an afternoon high tea!
An evening
Complete!
A day,
A tea walk, true,
A tea walk,
A learning, true!
A day of time,
My learning, true!

21. PROMISES ADORNING A BANK AND HEDGE!

Promises,
A spring,
Adorning a bank
Bunches of daffodils,
A bank, a corner
A Peek,
From a bridge top,
River, a reminder
Of a spring
Around,
Beauty,
Grace,
A season,
Spring!

Promises of a spring
Every
Only
For a task
A step light
For a completion
A daffodil,
An emblem
Of a promise
I signify
For a day of hard work,
Several daffodils
Promises
I choose
For a fulfillment
Of Several tasks!

A hedge,
A reminder,
A promise fulfilled,
A border complete,
A hedge!
Not any a space left
Adorning a bank,
My daffodils in full bloom!

22. WOODS, I UNDERSTAND A DAY

Woods,
I walk a few miles,
I understand a walk
A summer,
Trees,
Not my gold,
A green,
I need,
For a shade, a summer!
A cool breeze,
My face!
A comfort,
My walk!

My walk,
I understand,
A few branches, Roots, hanging down, A banyan tree?
A need to sit down,
Rest,
My Walk,
Only a comfort!

Woods,
A summer,
I understand,
A walk,
A joy!

23.   WOODS, A DAY OF POIGNANCY!

Woods!
Are you poignant?
A day of no breeze!
A calm,
A silence,
Not,
A smile,
Only A whisper,
Leaves awake,
Only In thought,
A thought, Only for a knowledge!

Woods,
Poignant,
I need to read
My book, my notes,
A focus,
For a meaning,
An understanding!
A solution,
I need to find!

24. WOODS, AN ODE, A DAY OF SONGS!

Woods,
I am her today,
A summer
Of my friends,
A songs,
I sing the day,
For a praise of
Your grace,
Your
Friendship,
Your
Sincerity,
Devotion,
Loyalty,
For the
Fruits,
Flowers,
Vegetables,
Harvest you
Best!
An ode to you,
My trees,
My friends!

25. WOODS, A SLANT, MY CREEPERS!

Woods A Musical Path!

Woods,
A slant,
A fall graceful,
my creepers!
A season,
A dark, a green, my maple leaf!
A light, a green, a flower, a hydrangea!
A slight, a summer, a green, a fern!
My creeper trellis,
A fall,
From atop,
Only a grace!

Woods A Musical Path,
A curve, a fold, a rose bud!
A grace, a twirl, a fold a peony!
A grace, an alternate, a leaf, a two!
A Jasmine , a Maruvam a weave, a line!
My grace,
Only smiles,
Every!

My birds,
Only
A whisper,
Every morning!
A message!
Woods,
A weave of a musical path,
Only true,
Every!
Oh, Woods

You are a mystery!
A path musical, every season!
How true!
You are beautiful!

Oh Woods,
How can I match,
Thee!
An art,
A weave,
A path for an art,
A season, every!

26. FALL BREEZE AND AUTUMN EXPRESSIONS

Autumn breeze,
An autumn grace!
Autumn folds,
A shape!
A color, a grace!

A purple,
A green,
A red!
A velvet, true!
A plush,
A decor!

An antique,
An ornate,
A jewel!
A bracelet,
A necklace,
An adornment!

An art,
A grace of colors!
Colors,
I match
An autumn!
My autumn flowers!
My autumn vegetables,
My autumn fruits!
A texture, a soft,
A weave, a thick,
A canvas,
A plain!
A color,
I match,
My autumn Art!

27. WINTER SNOW AND WINTER DAYS

Winter snow,
A snow,
A bed for days
Until a sunshine!
My winter days,
I reminisce!
Days of cheer,
I exude,
A book of poems,
I read!

Days I reminisce,
Only, memories,
An artsy twine
Of leaves, stories!
A few green,
Some yellow,
A few brown,
Stories of life, a season!

A green,
Memories, a joy!
Yellow,
A road,
I need to watch,
For An illness!
Brown,
Withered,
I need to clear a path,
Only,
For New beginnings!

28. LEAVES, A BREEZY FLUTTER!

Woods,
How doth
Thy wonders!
Not lonely,
You are,
Thy magnificence,
Not for a spoil, any!
Thou dost,
An arrangement!
A sparkle,
Thy leaves!
A winter!
Seasons,
Only a dream, true!
Thou ist
A hope!
A path,
I choose,
From many!
A line, true!

Not for a vain,
My smile,
For thee,
But, Only a grace!
I bestow thee,
A bow!
A gesture,
My hands, only for a help!
A piroutte,
A dance,
For a food I offer!
How doth thou?
But, How is thy wonder?

Only so beautiful,
Are Thy wonders,
Every a path,
A path,
I choose, a season,
Only for a grace!
Only for a
Path fulfilled!

29. AUTUMN NOT TO FALTER?

Woods,
An autumn,
Last,
I faltered!
A step,
Not right!
My art,
A ruin!
My flowers,
A disarray!
My eyes, wide,
Only bewildered!
Lips,
Only tight!
A falter,
I did not mean!

Woods,
A need,
I need to learn, true!

30. AUTUMN FRAGRANCE, EVERY AN AUTUMN!

An Autumn Fragrance,
Every An Autumn,
An autumn match,
Of a flower, leaf,
And an Autumn vegetable!

An Autumn fragrance,
An autumn corn,
An autumn pumpkin,
A fragrance, a match,
A leaf,
An orange, yellow!

An Autumn fragrance,
Autumn flowers,
Mums,
Daisies,
Pansies,
A match,
My Autumn Home!

My flowers,
Fruits,
Vegetables
An autumn,
A Fragrance,
A color,
A harmony!
An autumn fragrance,
A match, true!

31.   AN AUTUMN, NOT A SKIP!

An autumn,
I do not need to skip!
A step,
Or a half!
A measure,
Of an autumn walk,
For a right!

A winter,
Only a step less,
A support,
Of a step
For a walk!
An autumn,
I compare,
A winter,
My smiles!
A learning, true!

32.   AN ART, I COULD NOT FIND!

An art,
I carved,
A decor,
A canvas!

Did not find
Could not find
My canvas,
My art!

Several eyes missed this art!
An eye,
Not for a color,
Nor a pattern,
But only
For Sunrise,
And Sunset!
A carve,
Only,
Time, true!

An art,
A carve,
A devotion,
My prayers!

33. STORIES UNDER THE BANYAN TREE

Every a summer evening,
A banyan tree,
Is my
summer way!
A few,
Stories,
An evening,
To listen,
Under a banyan tree!
A way of a Summer life!

Summer friendships,
Summer gatherings,
A few,
Only to renew every summer!
A summer memory
I pen,
In my summer book
Of friendships!
Years of stories,
Under the banyan tree,
Summer memories,
I pass down,
To my own!

34. SUMMER SECRETS

Summer secrets,
Summer secrets,
A few, I found!
A path of woods,
A path, I picked!
Flowers,
A weave,
A bud and a leaf!
Leaves, colors, several trees!
Secrets,
I unfold!
My Memories
Of a day!
A weave of flowers,
Several a branch!
A few, a curve, a bun, a round!
Flowers a pair, an upside down!

A story of a secret!
A dusk,
A sunrise,
A path,
A difference!
A bud,
A leaf,
An ascent,
A difference, A height!

Leaves,
A wide,
A path,
A tree!
A wide, a path, several!
A round,
Only for dances of trees!
A breeze, my dance, true!

35.   AN AUTUMN SENSIBILITY

An autumn sensibility,
A look I need to wear!
A dress!
A skirt!
A plain!
A thick,
A texture,
A cut!
A collar,
A high!
A sleeve,
A full!

An autumn sensibility,
An expression
I need to wear!
Lips,
Not for any an expression!
Eyes,
Only for An Intelligence,
I need to see!
Not any an Expression,
For a hurry!
A walk, Straight!
A step, A pause,
Not For,
Until A need!

An autumn sensibility,
Only a pride, a respect,
Every an eye!
An autumn sensibility, Only true!

Only Smiles!
A summer, true!

36.   WOODS, A WILDERNESS

Woods,
How hath thou?
Not a path,
This season!
Trees overgrown!
Flowers, beds
Every a corner!
An acre,
A flower,
A type,
True?

Oh Woods,
How shalt thou?
How hath thee?
How can'st thou?
To create,
A path,
Of woods,
A season,
A work, true!
Only work, a devotion, a need!
A path, a need, only
For a walk,
Every a season!

Woods,
A wilderness,
I don't need to clear!
Only a path, I need,
For a walk!

Woods,
Tis this season,

There is no path!
Next,
An autumn,
Also?

A summer,
My walk of woods,
A path,
I missed!
A wilderness,
Only, True!

37. AN AUTUMN PRIDE

An autumn pride
An autumn pride,
An autumn I celebrate,
An autumn festival!
A day,
Of decor,
My home!
My autumn art,
This year,
An autumn jewel!
A purple amethyst,
A decor my
Windows!
My pumpkins,
Outside, My door,
For An autumn Auspicious Sacred!
An autumn,
I begin
My autumn prayers!
An autumn bell,
I ring before
And after my prayers!
An autumn chant,
A sunrise,
A sunset,
Only for
Blessings,
My family!

38. AN AUTUMN VINTAGE

An autumn vintage!
An autumn,
I show an autumn!
Visitors!

An autumn vintage dress,
A wine red,
Pleats, very thin,
For a fall!
A fall,
To grace my walk!
A dress,
To my knees,
For a respect!
A velvet wine,
A grace,
An evening!

An autumn decor vintage,
A decor,
A wine purple,
My flowers, roses!
A vintage collection!
A vase,
Only a dark red!

My front door,
An autumn vintage, decor!
Flowers, leaves,
A few stalks of hay!
Decorated on a
Vintage Plate,
An adornment,
My front door!

My autumn vintage,
An art
For an autumn match!
A season,
An autumn,
True!

39. A SUMMER, ONE A DAY!

A summer,
One every,
A day,
Only,
A few,
I work,
Puzzles,
Math,
To assemble
My words,
My math,
For a year of
Study at school!

A summer,
Onc a day,
Only a hurry,
I need to complete!

A hard work,
Of a year,
I nccd to
Divide,
A division
Only
To ease
My burden!

A summer, one a day,
Worthy,
My hard work!

40. AUTUMN BRANCHES, I SEE

An autumn,
Autumn branches,
Higher,
Every a branch,
I see!

A profile,
An autumn branch,
A slant,
An angle,
A difference!
Some a branch down,
A flower downcast!
Some, a branch high,
A bud,
I open!

An autumn branch,
A branch,
An art,
An autumn,
A view,
An autumn,
An art,
A match,
A decor,
My autumn home!

41. AN AUTUMN ANTIQUE, A TREASURE!

An autumn antique,
A treasure,
I open,
A wrap,
A velvet,
A silk cushion,
A deep purple diamond pendant,
Exquisite, a jewel!
Ear drops,
Small drops of purple jewels,
Only a shine
Afar, a sky
Stars of jewels,
An adornment,
My dress!

An autumn antique,
A treasure,
I wear with my dress
A purple deep,
Jewels, sparkles,
On my neck,
A few,
A decor,
My hands!
A shape,
A leaf,
Petals two!

42. A SUMMER, ANEW!

A summer,
Anew,
A difference,
A holiday,
An after,
I write my essay!

This summer,
An essay,
A difference,
A season!

A cheer,
A joy,
My essay!

A difference,
A friendship,
I made,
This summer!

A friendship,
A new,
A learning,
My mind!
Only for a learning more,
A renewal,
A summer, next!

A summer anew, true!

43. AN AUTUMN, A RENEWAL!

An autumn spice,
A renewal,
A new,
I blend,
Along
With an old,
A pepper,
A need,
A turmeric,
A fragrance,
A flavor rich,
All seasons,
A cinnamon,
A soup,
A blend
For my autumn squash soup!

Now,
An autumn
Renewal,
A need
For an autumn
Dish,
My renewal
Of an
Autumn soup,
And an
Autumn spice!
For an autumn meal,
Every an autumn!

44. A SPRING TROVE!

A spring trove,
A treasure,
I open,
A decor paper,
A Pink,
A decor paper,
A Green!

A pendant,
My daughter,
I gift,
A name,
A language, new!

A pendant,
My mother,
I gift,
A name, Mother,
A flower, new!

A spring trove,
A celebration,
My mother,
My daughter,
A family treasure,
A trove!

45. WOODS, A GROVE!

A new woods,
I walked!
Woods, a path,
Not any,

Woods,
Only a grove!
A grove of
Mangoes?

Mangoes,
Several a color,
Orange, green,
Small, big!
A grove,
Several apart,
A cluster of trees!

A cluster,
A few,
A path,
I weave,
A circle,
An ellipse,
True,
Woods,
A grove, a path!

46. WOODS, SEASONS!

Woods, Seasons,
I bestow you,
One, a time,
A year!
A Christmas!
Jewels,
I decorate!
Gifts,
I adorn,
Woods,
Trees, a fir,
A praise of you!

A Christmas tree,
A tree,
We adorn, gifts
Decorate, satin bows,
A purple,
Yellow,
Red or
Green,
Gifts
We exchange,
A family tradition,
A celebration
To strengthen
The bonds
Of a family!

A celebration
For a Christmas!

Woods,
A tree,
A joy,
A Christmas!

47.   WOODS, A PATH OF A BROOK!

Woods,
A path, a creek,
Long,
Narrow,
A zigzag,
A weave
Only to
Wind,
Around
A bridge!

An
Abrupt,
A Stop!

A path
I need?
A need only
To stop
Not a few drops,
But a river?

48. AN AUTUMN SKETCH

An Autumn Sketch,
I draw,
An autumn profile!
Sharp,
A goal defined!
Slice,
A cut,
For a finesse!
Stuffed,
A knowledge,
Met!

An autumn sketch,
A curve,
I revise,
Only for
A relation,
A definition,
I need to meet!

49. MY CARVE, I NEED TO KNOW

A carve,
I need to know
At the outset,
A beginning,
A carve,
An end a carve,
I need to know!

A story,
I need to write?

A story,
A few lines,
A paragraph,
A few pages,
For Any, I need,
An art,
An education
My work,
A fulfilment!

50.   AN AUTUMN KNOLL!

An autumn knoll,
A few,
A mile from my
Village!

An autumn knoll,
A season!
Flowers, deep
A decor, a border!
Purple mums,
Yellow marigolds,
Red roses
Cascades,
Of a weave,
A silk,
A gold,
A sunrise,
A center!

An autumn knoll,
I walk
Only for a change,
A sunset,
A difference,
An orange shade,
True,
An autumn season!

51.   A SPRING CLEAN!

A spring,
I clean my windows,
A glass,
A view,
I need to display
My flower pots,
My kitchen pots!

A day of a visitor,
I need to prepare for,
A pot of flowers,
White, pink, and yellow!

A grace of a visitor,
A kitchen kettle,
A kitchen teapot,
A white, a canvas!
Roses, pink a decor!
A sparkling white!

My spring clean,
Only a spring afresh true!

52. WOODS, A WAY TO A PATH

Woods,
A path,
I need to choose,
For my goals!

A path,
Not a stop,
But a path
Only to continue!

A path,
Only to grow,
A path
Of kindness,
Grace,
Devotion,
Commitment,
Loyalty,
Sincerity!
All,
Only for a path,
Of
Prosperity!

53. SPRING DAFFODILS!

Spring daffodils,
Several lines,
Several acres,
A garden?
A farm!

Daffodils,
Every a stem,
A peek,
A friendship
Until a summer,
An end!

An alternate arrangement
A yellow,
A white
A yellow, orange,
A spring festival!
Daffodils,
A light spring breeze,
New dresses,
My daffodils, a spring,
Clouds, a difference!
A color of a sky,
My Daffodil breeze!
A color, true, a breeze!
A celebration
Of my spring harvest!
My spring daffodils,
I say thee,
You are beautiful!

54. A VASE OF DAFFODILS

A vase,
I arrange,
My daffodils,
A, Cut a size,
A difference,
A flower,
A side!

A flower,
An arrangement,
A face,
A side!
A face down,
A flower,
A droop!
A vase,
My daffodils
Only a carve
An art,
An arrangement,
A spring!

55. WOODS, A SEASON, A COLOR, I CARVE!

Woods,
A season, an autumn,
Colors, a few,
I choose!

A color
I use
To dress my
God, A silk!
This year,
A purple gold!
A yellow gold!
A orange gold!
A day
Of navaratri,
I celebrate!

A prayer,
I chant,
A sunrise,
Sunset!
Woods,
A color,
I chose,
For Three days of
Navaratri!

56. AN AUTUMN PRIDE!

An autumn pride,
An autumn pride,
My autumn food,
I cook
My family!

A squash,
Orange,
Tomato,
Peppers,
Onions,
And spices,
I blend!
A green,
A red,
A pepper,
A flavor,
My meal!

My autumn radish,
A salad
A blend my
Lemon juice,
A peanut powder,
A seasoning,
A mustard,
A hing,
Only delicious!

My autumn corns,
A bake dry
My oven,
A spice,
I blend,
A cumin salt,

A butter fragrance,
I blend,
For
An autumn warmth!

57. A TREE, A BRANCH, A COLOR!

An autumn,
My tree,
Only,
empty!
Leaves, orange, yellow, red and brown,
My carpet of woods,
A color,
To stay an autumn,
Until a winter!

Tis this season,
Autumn,
Branches,
Several a color!
A light yellow, a color, an autumn ready!
An orange, round, an, autumn ripe!
A brown, ready, a winter, true!
only a fall a branch, a mid-autumn

A yellow,
An orange,
I need to
Know,
A difference,
Of a season!

A branch I carve,
Several I carve,
A difference,
A season,
A difference,
A color!

58.   DROPS, SEVERAL A SHAPE!

Rain drops,
Several, a shape,
Several, a season!

A color, similar
A difference,
A volume!
A drop,
A small,
A hold, true!
A large,
A drop,
A run,
A truth!

Drops small,
A jewel,
An adornment,
My ears!

Drops large,
A jewel,
An adornment,
My dress!

!

59.   NOT TO WASTE ANY!

Not to waste, A time,
Any,
A morning,
A note,
I read, to complete, A task!
An afternoon, A note,
I read,
To think, and Carve!

Several, Mistakes,
My home,
I need to mend!
A fault!
A meal,
For a liking!
A fault,
I need to coach, My kids,
Any, A subject!
A fault,
I need to Arrange,
My home better!
An evening, A meal,
I cook,
For
An evening meal,
A togetherness,
A cheer, every!
A smile,
A laughter,
My family!
My smile, Only a joy!
A home,
A family, Only Kind, Helpful, Sincere,

Devoted, Loyal!
A togetherness, A walk true,
A difference,
A mother!

60. A MOTHER, A VIEW OF A DAUGHTER!

A mother,
A view of a door,
of a daughter,
An inside,
A view,
A daughter,
Healthy,
Cheerful,
Helpful,
Affectionate,
Intelligent!
A view outside,
A daughter,
A friend trustworthy,
A family,
A whole!

A togetherness,
A family,
Precious,
A daughter!

61. A CORN MAZE, CORNS A DIFFERENCE?

A corn maze,
I walk,
Corn stalks dry,
Corn stalks, yellow,
Corn stalk white, faded,
Corn stalks, green, afresh
A difference,
A harvest!

A harvest,
A rich yellow, a corn
A green, a cover!

An after,
Only
Cornstalks dry,
A farm!

A corn maze,
A difference,
A walk, seasons!

62.   A FLOWER, A PATTERN I ARRANGE!

A flower,
A pattern,
I arrange,
A pattern, lines orange and brown, for a sunrise,
A pattern, plain, a white, mid-afternoon,
A pattern, a shadow, an autumn morning,
A pattern, only a gold, orange (doddu malle), a jasmine!

A pattern,
A season,
A flower arrangement, true!

A skill,
A job,
A work,
I perfect,
A carve, true,
An arrangement
Of an art, true!

63.   A SOLITUDE, A NEED!

A solitude,
A need,
A few!

A need,
To think!
A solution,
To a problem,
A carve,
Only Better,
A solution found!

A sorrow,
A sadness,
Only to see
A memory fade!
A Tree,
A flower,
A leaf,
Afresh,
My mind,
My thoughts,
Only afresh,
Anew!

64.   A CONVERSATION, AWRY!

A conversation,
A begin,
Only
For a topic,
shared,
For a time spent,
A rejoice, a memory!

A conversation,
For not any a topic,
Only a fault,
I find,
A conversation,
I leave,
Alone a bliss!

My book,
A conversation,
I read,
Not any a
Fault,
Or,
I falter!

A conversation,
Awry,
Not awry,
A solitude!
A devotion,
For a prayer,
A book,
An art,
Only
For a mind at rest!

65. A GRASS, A WALK A DIFFERENCE!

A grass,
A green,
I walk a summer,
My footsteps,
Soft,
A step,
A mile,
my walk,
Only a grace!

A walk, a falter,
An autumn,
My shoes,
A support,
A few steps,
A mile!
A step
A measure,
Not for a fall!

Footsteps, I count,
Only for a
A day
I save
A fall!

66.   A CURVE, A DIFFERENCE!

A curve,
A difference,
A season,
A measure,
A new,
true!

67.   MY WOES, A DAY, AWAY!

My woes, a day, away!
A woe,
A day,
A need to understand!
A woe
For
Not to create!
A woe, Begun,
A woe, Lost,
Only a joy!
A woe,
Not A difference,
I need to understand!
A woe,
I know now!
A woe,
I understood,
Is a woe, Begone!
A woe,
I do not create,
Not a woe!

68. A CURTAIN, I NEED TO UNDERSTAND

A curtain,
I need to understand,
A curtain of respect,
A home!
A respect of,
A Shelter,
Clothing,
Food,
And
Kindness!

A curtain,
I need to understand,
A curtain,
A weave!
A chintz,
A velvet,
A chiffon!
Only,
A grace,
A decor,
A decency,
A home!

69.   A TREE, A SKIRT, A PATTERN!

A tree,
Branches, a few,
A skirt!
A billow,
A skirt,
Branches up!
A skirt down,
Branches down!

A skirt a fall, a grace,
Only for a dance, a pirouette!

A skirt,
A grace,
A lady!

A walk,
A difference,
A skirt
A pleat!

A walk
Only
For a grace, true!

70. NOT A WEAR A DRESS!

A dress,
I wear for a day,
A year!
Several years,
Several seasons,
A dress,
Not a wear!
My marriage,
Only a reminder,
Of my dress!
A year old!

My dress!
A day,
A year,
A celebration,
Of my marriage anniversary!

Every, a year
A dress,
I wear,
Not a wear,
Even now!

71. A PRESENCE ONLY WANTED!

A presence,
I await,
Every,
A conversation,
Only, a learning,
A new knowledge,
A need
For a use!

A presence,
I await,
A look only beautiful,
Any,
An occasion!

A presence,
I await,
Creative,
A leader,
Every,
An interaction!

A presence wanted,
At all times!

72. A SKILL, A SUCCESS, MY CONFIDENCE!

A confidence,
I define,
A word for success!
A skill,
I master,
A subject!
A conversation,
I lead, a topic,
A work,
I craft,
With penmanship!

A boon,
My skill!
For a skill
I exhibit,
Only
A success,
My way!

73. A SILENCE, I LEARN

A silence,
A need,
To learn,
I need to read,
And
Understand!
To write on paper,
My learning,
A support, a learning,
Of An example,
Written!
Not an option,
To miss,
A learning, written!

An acquiescence,
Of A learning, true,
A grade,
A letter, An 'A'!

A silence,
A need,
Any,
A devotion
For a task!

A disturbance,
By any,
I need to To avoid,
For a learning, true,
Only, Woods,
A comfort!

74.   A TRAIL OF YELLOW LEAVES, A BRANCH

A trail of yellow leaves,
A branch,
An autumn,
A begin!

A trail,
A yellow,
A scarf,
I wear
Around
My neck,
A grace,
An autumn!

POETRY CLASSICS

PATRIOTIC SONG OF USA

My Country, I appreciate you!
My Country, I support you!
A voice in unity of words
For Success,
Is the strength of our nation!

We uphold the values of the constitution of our country!
We embody the values of unity in strength.
We support the values of Loyalty, Trust, Faith and devotion in
everything we do!
We the people of this country are one family!
We support diversity of cultures for
Values of Peace and Harmony.
Patriotism is the strength of our nation

My country, I support you in good and bad times!
My country, I am proud of you!
My country, I belong to this nation!
My country Is my family!
Peace and Harmony is an emblem of our Country!

SECTION 2

MUSICAL ALBUM, SPRING REVOIR.

BUDS A SUNRISE

Buds, I am a fold A sunrise go :low to high
G5F5E5D5C5B4A4G4

Awake a few, flowers a sunset: high to low
F4G4A4B4C5 C5B4A4G4

A flower, a bud, a leaf a twine
E5D5C5B4A4G4F4

A green, a spring, a star!
E4F4G4A4B4C5

Buds a few,
E5D5C5
Flowers a few,
E5D5C5
A few, a flower, an art for time!
D5C5B4A4G4F4E4

Buds I am a fold A sunrise
G5F5E5D5C5B4A4G4
Awake a few, flowers a sunset!
F4G4A4B4C5 C5B4A4G4

Buds, a color, a note a blend!
E5D5C5B4A4G4F4
A red, a purple a season a twine!
E4F4G4A4B4C5B4A4G4F4

Buds a fold,
E5D5C5
Buds a weave
E5D5C5
A few a color, an art for time!
E5D5C5B4A4G4F4E4

A bud I am a day,
C5E5 D5C5B4A4G4F4
A flower I am a night,
E4F4G4A4B4C5

A few, a day, a breeze, a night!
E4F4G4A4B4C5

Buds, I seek thee!
E5D5C5
Flowers, I seek thee!
E5D5C5
My buds, my flowers, a season I seek!
E5D5C5B4A4G4F4E4

My Buds,
C5D5
My Flowers,
B4A4
A weave for time!
G4F4E4D4

1. SPRING WALK

Walking in the woods,
A day of spring,
Looking for a blossom,
March, a spring friend!

Oh a spring daisy laughter
Ah a spring lily, yellow!
OOO sunrise a smile!
Umm sunset a Hee!

Walking on a path,
A trail of daisies
Looking for a cove,
A summer cove, my friend

Oh an autumn pumpkin beam!
Oh an autumn orange brown!
OOO an autumn pumpkin scarecrow!
Umm an autumn sunset cider!

Walking…

2.   A SUMMER LINE

Summers, a season,
E5D5 C5(2 times)
Summer, colors my smile!
C5D5B5F5G5A5

Summer days of dreams,
E4F4G4A4G4
Summer days of smiles,
E4F4G4A4G4
Summer lines of flowers!
E4F4G4A4G4

Summer days......
E4F4G4
Summer skies...
E4F4G4
A Summer!
F4 E4(2 times)

Summers a day, Summer days, I skip
E5 D5(2) C5B4, B4 A4(2 times)
A4 G4(2 times) F4 E4
Summer skies of summers!
E4F4G4A4G4

Summer days of peace
E4F4G4A4G4
Summer days of calm
E4F4G4A4G4
Summer flowers of summer!
E4F4G4A4G4

3.   FRIENDS FOR DAYS

Friends for days
Friends a few
A family for life!

A family a few,
A harmony for time!
Peace, every,
A family I cherish!

Passed, a season,
Time, a day, a few,
A day anew,
Time, a way, a path,
Only To understand, a day of life!
Time, a friend, a family for life!

Friends for days
Friends a few
A family for life!

4.   FELL A FEW A DRIZZLE

Fell a few,
A drizzle,
A pour,
A Day of autumn!

A drizzle, a pour,
A giggle my buds,
A drizzle, a slant,
A laughter, my flowers

Fell a few
A few, a season!
A few, a drops, of brook!

A return of autumn,
My colors of autumn!

A day of pour,
Afresh an autumn!
My flowers and leaves,
Afresh
An autumn!

A drizzle, a sky,
A color, a grey,
An orange, a violet, a blue, a rainbow, afar!

A day of drizzle,
Afresh,
My path,
A day of autumn,
Spring,
An autumn!

5. SUNRISE SUNSET AN ORANGE GOLD

Sunrise Sunset an orange gold
A few, until A!

Sunrise, a blue,
A few, a white, an artsy line!
Sunset, a gold,
Summer a color
A few, a line, an orange art!

Come again, a summer!
Come again!
Come a-g-a-i-n!
A season, A summer!

Sunrise, Sunset an orange gold
A few, until A!

Sunrise skies, a sunrise prayer,
Sunset skies, a sunset calm,
Sunrise sunset, a harmony!

Sunrise, a seasonal summer
Sunset, a season, an art!

Sunrise Sunset an orange gold
A few, until A!

6. EVERY AN AUTUMN, AN AUTUMN ART TRUE!

Every an autumn,
An autumn art true!

Art, an autumn, season, a path,
Sacred, an autumn, a prayer!
Blessing, an autumn, a day!
An autumn, a day, an auspicious!
Prayers I fulfill thee!

Prayers, a name!
Prayers, a chant!
Sacred, a name, an autumn day!

Every An autumn,
An autumn Art, true!

Tradition, an autumn custom!
Celebration, an autumn festival!
Auspicious, an autumn day!

Flowers, I bestow!
Leaves, I bestow!
Sacred, a wish, an autumn auspicious day!

Every An autumn,
An autumn Art, true!

7. AUTUMN, A SUNSET!

Autumn,
A sunset,
A match,
My autumn corns,

Autumn, an art, a twirl, an autumn ivy!
Autumn, an autumn color, an autumn day a theme!

Autumn, a way of,
Autumn, a day of,
Autumn Art, my day!

Autumn,
A sunrise,
A match,
My autumn pumpkins!

Autumn, a circle, an autumn pumpkin a carve!
Autumn, an art, my autumn lights, an autumn cart!

Autumn, a song,
Autumn, a note,
Autumn, a match,
An autumn sacred song!

Autumn,
A sunset,
A match,
My autumn corns!

8. FOR TIME YOU ARE A PART OF MY LIFE!

Spring, a day of Roses light,
Spring, a first, a day of sunlight!
Spring, a few, leaves, a branch!
For time, a flower, a beauty of a season!

Spring, a herb of grace!
Spring, a season of tea!

Spring a way, a path, true!
Spring, a day, a weave, light!

Spring, A spring afresh!
Spring, roses, my garden!
For time, a leaf, sacred an autumn!

Spring, awake, a new, a sunrise!
Spring, away, a new, a summer!
Spring, for time!
Spring for new!
Spring a path, a weave, a four!
Spring a flower!
Spring a dress!
Spring a weave, similar a season!
For time, spring a weave, praiseworthy

SECTION 3
BAVAVOVUE IN DURVUE

GODDESS VISALAKOVUE VISALAKOVUE BAVOVUE –

110 NAMES (MOTHER PRAYERS)

1. suwervei, anikachamantovue avovue! (Goddess, a new name of a flower, chamanti, another name of Goddess Durga)
2. suwervei, upakaouvue avovue! (useful)
3. suwervei, dhanouvue avovue! (Prosperity)
4. suwervei, paropakaovue avovue! (Helpful)
5. suwervei, sahanaovue avovue! (patience)
6. suwervei, kutumbaovue avovue! (Family)
7. suwervei, prasannaovue avovue! (praise)
8. suwervei, kashtasukovue avovue! (Good and bad times)
9. suwervei, bandhovue avovue! (Relations)
10. suwervei, subakaryaovue avovue! (new beginnings)
11. suwervei, dhanyaouve avovue! (Grains)
12. suwervei, raagovue avovue! (Raga)
13. suwervei, namartaouve avovue! (Soft mild)
14. suwervei, saantavovue! (Peaceful)
15. suwervei, akaasaouve avovue! (Sky)
16. suwervei, vaanouve avovue! (Rain)
17. suwervei, pallaovue avovue! (Fruits)
18. suwervei, sarvaouve avovue! (All)
19. suwervei, upassouve avovue! (Devotee)
20. suwervei, sahanaouvue avovue! (Tolerance)
21. suwervei, panchamiovue avovue! (Good Star)
22. suwervei Samsarouve (family relation) avovue
23. suwervei, sarvasampurnouvue avovue! (All ways good)

24. suwervei, manchiovue! (Very nice)

25. suwervei, matruaouvue avovue! (Motherly)

26. suwervei, punyamouvue avovue! (Blessed)

27. suwervei, suprasnouve avovue! (Very Pleasant)

28. suwervei, gandaouve avovue! (Fragrance full)

29. suwervei, nischitaovue avovue! (Committed)

30. suwervei, nijamouve avovue! (Truthful)

31. suwervei, pratibhaovue avovue! (Peaceful)

32. suwervei, dhyryaovue avovue! (Courage)

33. suwervei, dayamouve avovue! (Considerate)

34. suwervei, danaouve avovue! (Charitable)

35. suwervei, kaantaouve avovue! (Light)

36. suwervei, bhadyatouve avovue! (Reponsible)

37. suwervei, buddhibalamovue avovue! (Wisdom)

38. suwervei, gyaanaovue avovue! (Knowledge)

39. suwervei, aakaouvue avovue!

40. suwervei, purnimaovue avovue! (Full Moon)

41. suwervei, suryaovue avovue! (Sunrise)

42. suwervei, maanaouvue avovue! (human)

43. suwervei, puvvaovue avovue! (Flower)

44. suwervei, mallikaovue avovue! (fruit)

45. suwervei, pataouvue avovue! (Song)

46. suwervei, ammaovue avovue! (Mother)

47. suwervei, putrikaovue avovue! (Daughter)

48. suwervei, ragaovue avovue! (musical notes)

49. suwervei, Puvupaliouve avovue! (As pure as a flower and milk)

50. suwervei, panchamruvouve avovue! (As swee as Honey)

51. suwervei, satyaouve avovue! (Truthful)

52. suwervei, kamalouve avovue! (Grace of a lotus)

53. suwervei, amrudraksavaouve avovue! (A honey nectar of grapes)

54. suwervei, prakritaovue avovue! (Nature)

55. suwervei, vidyabaovue avovue! (Education)

56. suwervei, nirmalovue avovue! (Serene)

57. suwervei, nishkalaovue avovue! (Flawless)

58. suwervei, kutumbaouve avovue! (Family type)

59. suwervei, sahayamovue avovue! (Helpful)

60. suwervei, nidanaovue avovue! (peaceful)
61. suwervei, kumkumovue avovue! (A bindi signifies a married lady)
62. suwervei, pasupovue avovue! (Wear a sacred yellow thread)
63. suwervei, sraddaovue avovue! (Focus)
64. suwervei, dharmaovue avovue! (Right Path)
65. suwervei, dhyvabkatovue avovue! (Devotion to God)
66. suwervei, sakramovue avovue! (Correctly done)
67. suwervei, sadgunovue avovue! (Only good values)
68. suwervei, uttamovue avovue! (Only good thoughts)
69. suwervei, sevaovue avovue! (Caring)
70. suwervei, vinayaovue avovue! (Humble)
71. suwervei, nidambarovue avovue! (Modest)
72. suwervei, mechukovue avovue! (Appreciative)
73. suwervei, ishtaovue avovue! (Likeable)
74. suwervei, sampradapvue avovue! (Prosperous)
75. suwervei, manavasutraovue avovue! (Good Principles)
76. suwcrvci, Manokamovuc avovue! (Good Wishes)
77. suwervei, Siddhiovue avovue! (Success)
78. suwervei, abilsaovue avovue! (Hope)!
79. suwervei, nyayaovue avovue! (Just)
80. suwervei, Samanatovue avovue! (Equal)
81. suwervei, manovovue avovue! (Humanity)
82. suwervei, Durgaovue avovue! (Goddess Durga)
83. suwervei, Sampurnovue avovue! (Content)
84. suwervei, nitulovue avovue! (Adherence to code of conduct and rules)
85. suwervei, visalalakshimalliovue avovue! (A new name of Chamanti flower)
86. suwervei, Sukaovue avovue! (Comfort)
87. suwervei, Anukaovue avovue! (Submissive)
88. suwervei, namaskaovue avovue! (hands together)
89. suwervei, akasamouvue avovue! (Respect of Sky)
90. suwervei, bhumaovue avovue! (Respect of Earth
91. suwervei, abhayaovue avovue! (Not afraid)
92. suwervei, ikyatovue avovue! (Unity in all)

93. suwervei, Soukyamovue avovue! (Comfort of words or any)
94. suwervei, bhavaovue avovue! (Expressions)
95. suwervei, parampaovue avovue! (Customs)
96. suwervei, ritiaovue avovue! (Traditions)
97. suwervei, manasantovue avovue! (Peace of mind)
98. suwervei, Manchimansovue avovue! (Good Mind)
99. suwervei, ekagraovue avovue! (Anything for everyone's benefit)
100. suwervei, maataovue avovue! (Mother)
101. suwervei, pitaaovue avovue! (Father)
102. suwervei, Guruvaovue avovue! (Teacher)
103. suwervei, shisyaovue avovue! (Student)
104. suwervei, gauravaovue avovue! (Respect)
105. suwervei, samsaraovue avovue! (Children)
106. suwervei, banduaouve avovue! (Relations)
107. suwervei, sodarovue avovue! (Sisterly)
108. suwervei, nisabdaovue avovue! (Silence)
109. suwervei, harmoniovue avovue! (harmonious)
110. Suverwei Samptrutaovue (Content in life) avovue

Anikaouve dwashaouve **110 (Ladies Prayers)**
A girl must pray for all these qualities of life

1. suwervei, andamovue avovue! (Beautiful)
2. suwervei, naliovue avovue! (Graceful)
3. suwervei, dayaovue avovue! (Kind)
4. suwervei, namovue avovue! (all names)
5. suwervei, nammiovue avovue! (Trustworthy)
6. suwervei, nichpataovue avovue! (Sincere)
7. suwervei, viswaovue avovue! (Loyal)
8. suwervei, runaouve avovue! (Grafeful)
9. suwervei, sampurnaovue avovue! (Content)
10. suwervei, dhanaovue avovue! (Rich)
11. suwervei, samsarovue avovue! (Family life)
12. suwervei, vidyaovue avovue! (Education)
13. suwervei, saantaovue avovue! (Peaceful)
14. suwervei, garvaovue avovue! (Proud)
15. suwervei, dhyryaovue avovue! (Courage)
16. suwervei, vijawaovue avovue! (Succeed)
17. suwervei, sarvaovue avovue! (All virtues)
18. suwervei, sampurnovue avovue (Completed all)
19. suwervei, bhaktaovue avovue! (Devoted)
20. suwervei, punyaovue avovue!(Blessed)
21. suwervei, vijayaovue avovue! (Successful)
22. suwcrvci, nityasadhaovuc avovue! (Always hardworking)
23. suwervei, ratnamanovue avovue! (A jewel)
24. suwervei, karyasidhovue avovue! (Successful in all endeavors)
25. suwervei, kirtaovue avovue! (Good Reputation)
26. suwervei, gyanaovue avovue! (Knowledge)
27. suwervei, santosaovue avovue! (Happiness)
28. suwervei, uttamovue avovue! (Worthy)
29. suwervei, satyaovue avovue! (Truthful)
30. suwervei, viswasaovue avovue! (Loyal)
31. suwervei, vigyanaovue avovue! (Wisdom)
32. suwervei, sarvaswovue avovue! (All Qualities)
33. suwervei, dhyanomovue avovue! (Meditation)

34. suwervei, gunavanouvue avovue! (Only Good qualities)
35. suwervei, susilaovue avovue! (well natured)
36. suwervei, namratovue avovue! (Obedient)
37. suwervei, nibbatovue avovue! (Committed)
38. suwervei, viluveiovue avovue! (Valuable)
39. suwervei, naipunaovue avovue! (Skilled)
40. suwervei, pravinovue avovue! (Proficient)
41. suwervei, gyanaovue avovue! (Knowledge)
42. suwervei, televeiovue avovue! (Intelligent)
43. suwervei, mruduvaovue avovue! (Soft)
44. suwervei, neraveraovue avovue! (Fulfill)
45. suwervei, karyasiddaovue avovue! (Success in endeavors)
46. suwervei, kutumbaovue avovue! (Family bonding)
47. suwervei, nirmalovue avovue! (Serene)
48. suwervei, sadgunaovue avovue! (All qualities)
49. suwervei, bhaktaovue avovue! (Devoted)
50. suwervei, matruaovue avovue! (Motherly)
51. suwervei, ashtaiswarovue avovue! (All ways prosperous)
52. suwervei, suprasnovue avovue! (Very Pleasant)
53. suwervei, nityasantoshovue avovue! (Always Happy)
54. suwervei, sraddovue avovue! (Focus)
55. suwervei, naipunyovue avovue! (Skilled)
56. suwervei, sambandovue avovue! (Relation)
57. suwervei, nirvahanouve avovue!
58. suwervei, sarasvatovue avovue! (Education)
59. suwervei, asweeradovue avovue! (Blessings)
60. suwervei, akhilovue avovue! (Courageous)
61. suwervei, sarvagunovue avovue! (All qualities, an embodiment)
62. suwervei, nrityavovue avovue! (Dance)
63. suwervei, ullasouve avovue! (Cheerful)
64. suwervei, namaskaovue avovue! (Prayer)
65. suwervei, bhavaovue avovue! (Expressions)
66. suwervei, anukovue avovue! (Gentle and soft spoken)
67. suwervei, Pallavoue avovue! (Fruits)
68. suwervei, Pulaovue avovue! (Flowers)
69. suwervei, santaovue avovue! (Peaceful)

70.   suwervei, teneouve avovue! (Honey)
71.   suwervei, anikaovue avovue! (Beautiful)
72.   suwervei, balamovue avovue! (Strong)
73.   suwervei, buddhibalamovue avovue! (Behavior)
74.   suwervei, sundarovue avovue! (Beautiful)
75.   suwervei, vajraovue avovue! (Diamonds)
76.   suwervei, Kempaovue avovue! (Gems)
77.   suwervei, mutyaovue avovue! (Pearls)
78.   suwervei, mangalamovue avovue! (Prayer)
79.   suwervei, garvaovue avovue! (Pride)
80.   suwervei, gaanovue avovue! (Singing)
81.   suwervei, nrutyaovue avovue! (Dancing)
82.   suwervei, kumkamovue avovue! (Kumkuma)
83.   suwervei, stanaovue avovue! (Bindi)
84.   suwervei, Dharmouve avovue! (Right Path)
85.   suwervei, guruvaovue avovue! (Respect of Teacher
86.   suwervei, sishyaovue avovue! (Respect of Student)
87.   suwervei, dharmaovue avovue! (Correct Path)
88.   suwervei, kalyanovue avovue! (A Path of marriage)
89.   suwervei, suryaovue avovue! (Sunrise)
90.   suwervei, sanubhutiovue avovue! (Empathy)
91.   suwervei, chandraovue avovue! (Moon)
92.   suwervei, kaanukaovue avovue! (Gift)
93.   suwervei, satyaovue avovue! (Truth)
94.   suwervei, kalaovue avovue! (Art)
95.   suwervei, pravinyaovue avovue! (Expertise)
96.   suwervei, krushiovue avovue! (Hard Work)
97.   suwervei, chanchalaovue avovue! (Lively)
98.   suwervei, kusuma avovue! (Gentle)
99.   suwervei, dhanadhanyovue avovue! (Prosperous)
100. suwervei, prasannaovue avovue! (Happy)
101. suwervei, neipunyaovue avovue! (Skilled)
102. suwervei, poojaovue avovue! (Prayer)
103. suwervei, amrutamovue avovue! (Delicious)
104. suwervei, kantaovue avovue! (Light)
105. suwervei, parijatovue avovue! (Flowers of Parvati)

106. suwervei, madhurovue avovue! (Good Voice)
107. suwervei, sarvalakshanaovue avovue! (All good qualities)
108. suwervei, sarvadeviaovue avovue! (Devotion to all Gods)
109. suwervei, sraddaouve avovue! (Focus)
110. suverwei prasantaovue avovue

SECTION 4

PRAYERS IN NEW LANGUAGE DURVUE.

PRAYERS OF SINCERITY

Iau avum tieve sucavue
Tievum auv evu davovue
Ovue lieovue
I am sincere in all my endeavors!

Iau evu auvesicere imu allev mieve Evamervue

My prayers of Sincerity!
Mieuve Pravouve, ovue auvesicere!

Today and every day
Tievum anuv evow davovue

I work hard for success!
Iau heva tieve sucavue

I am sincere in all my endeavors!
Iau auvesicere imu allev mieve Evamervue

Please bless me God with success!
Pleauce besauve mieve Goem sucavue!

PRAYERS OF GRATITUDE

I am grateful for all bestowed upon me
Iau emu gravouvem fov allev besauve
Uvo mieve!

I am very much appreciative and thankful
In life!

Iau emu bev sauve lavier anou tauve imu viel!

Please bless me with success!
Pleauce besavue mieve wie sucavue!

ARATI PRAYERS

Auve Suverwei, pasapovue, lavello(Yellow)
Auve Suverwei, kumkaovue, reio (red)
Auve Suverwei Gandaovue hies (Brown)
Auve Suverwei Akshatovue siev (rice)

Samarpayami
Samarpovue (bestow!) Goem!

chamantovue
malleovue
I bestow thee
Samarpovue allev

dipaovue, nrutyaovue, gaanovue Samarpovue

Peauce mieve dauvovue

Something of a day, that's true!

A TRIBUTE TO A FATHER

Aau teraveovue tiev aau favovuer

A Father
Aau favovuer
A memory
Aau memorovue
I cherish
Iau ceherovue
An advice of
Avoun cavacovue ovue
kindness in words
Sivenovue liev woraovue!
And deeds!
Anou beveeovue!
Self less
Kavasouve
Of bestowing
Ovue jesieveon
Endless service!
Leveser sevierovue
For to see
Fov tov seouvue
Aau favovuer
A joy
Tev jeouvue!
And happiness
Anou Kevierovue
Of others
Ovue Mouve
Is the essence of life
Sau tev cevisouve ovue liveiovue

Printed in the United States
by Baker & Taylor Publisher Services